Encounters

The Epistle of Paul
the Apostle to the
GALATIANS

Encounters with God

The Epistle of Paul the Apostle to the GALATIANS

Copyright © 2008 by

Henry Blackaby, Th.M., D.D.
Richard Blackaby, M.Div., Ph.D.
Thomas Blackaby, M.Div., D.Min.
Melvin Blackaby, M.Div., Ph.D.
Norman Blackaby, M.Div., B.L., Ph.D.

Published by Thomas Nelson, Inc., P.O. Box 141000, Nashville, Tennessee 37214.

Scripture quotations are taken from The New King James Version® (NKJV), copyright 1979, 1980, 1982, 1992 Thomas Nelson, Inc., Publishers.

Library of Congress Cataloging-in-Publication Data
ISBN 1-4185-26460

Printed in the United States of America

08 09 10 11 RRD 9 8 7 6 5 4 3 2 1

All Scripture references are from the New King James Version of the Bible.

CONTENTS

AN INTRODUCTION TO THE EPISTLE OF GALATIANS

The Book of Galatians is an "epistle"—a formal letter intended to give instruction. The letter was written by the apostle Paul to the first-century churches in the region of Galatia, a province on the peninsula of Asia Minor.

The letter is one of twelve epistles written by the apostle Paul. We know that the recipients were Galatians, but there is uncertainty as to which "inhabitants of Galatia" Paul intended to address. If the letter was written to churches founded by Paul on his first missionary journey to South Galatia, then the date of the letter would be 48-50 AD, making this one of the earliest writings of Paul. Cities in South Galatia include Derbe, Lystra, Iconium, and Antioch—all a part of the Roman province of Galatia.

Some have contended that the Galatians were the Gauls located in northern Asia Minor, an area which the Gauls had invaded in the third century before Christ. Cities in this area include Pessinus, Ancrya, and Tavium. A trip to this area is not mentioned in the Book of Acts, yet it is conceivable that Paul evangelized this region on his second missionary journey, which would set the date of the letter no earlier than 52 AD and possibly as late as 57 AD.

Either way, this letter to the Galatians reflects Paul at his passionate, straightforward, and insightful best. False teachers had infiltrated the Galatian churches, introducing a corrupt Gospel message. Paul's stern tone was not a reflection of anger, but of intense love. He makes a case for his apostolic authority and urges the Galatians to heed his instruction: salvation is the result of faith, not works.

At the heart of the letter to the Galatians is the issue of circumcision. Legalistic Jewish Christians were insisting that the Gentile converts undergo this Jewish rite in order to become full members of God's family. Circumcision had come to be regarded by the Jewish Christians as a "sign" associated with salvation, and therefore a requirement for salvation. Paul stated clearly that no one is saved by the law or good deeds. Salvation is by faith in Jesus Christ alone.

Paul traces the Old Testament roots of the Gospel—especially the faith of Abraham—and states the purpose of the law, all as a backdrop for his admonition to avoid the extremes of both legalism and liberty.

Since the time of the Protestant Reformation, many have called Galatians "Luther's book," because its forceful argument about salvation was used extensively by Luther as a foundational stone for Reformation theology.

The letter is written in the form of Roman correspondence, with Paul clearly "autographing" the letter at its beginning and end (See Galatians 1:1 and 5:2). Most of Paul's letters have an introductory statement of thanksgiving. This one does not, which may indicate the severity of the situation in Galatia and Paul's urgency in writing.

About the Author, the Apostle Paul. Paul's name was originally Saul (Acts 13:9), the royal name of Israel's first king. Upon his conversion, he adopted the name Paul, which literally meant "little" and reflected his self-evaluation as being "the least of the apostles" (1 Corinthians 15:9). For certain, in the history of Christianity, the "little" apostle became the foremost apostle to the Gentile world.

Paul was a Roman citizen, his hometown being Tarsus, the chief city of Cilicia. He was fluent in Greek, studied philosophy and theology under Gamaliel, and was also a Hebrew, the son of a Pharisee from the tribe of Benjamin. Paul, too, became a Pharisee, a very strict follower of Jewish religious laws. By trade, he was a tentmaker. This unique blend of cultural, religious, and experiential factors gave Paul unusual entrée into both Gentile and Jewish circles.

Initially, Paul was a major force in denouncing Christianity in Jerusalem, and had been a willing witness to Stephen's martyrdom. While on a mission to seek out and destroy Christians who had traveled to Syria, Paul had a dramatic encounter with the risen Christ and, in the aftermath, became as zealous a believer in Christ Jesus and advocate for the Gospel as he once had been a zealous foe to the early church. He took several fruitful and demanding missionary journeys, spending as long as two years in some areas to teach those who had heeded the Gospel message and accepted Jesus as their Savior. Over the decades of his ministry, he became the most influential church planter and theologian in the early church. His letters addressed both the triumphs and difficulties encountered by the first-century Christians, many of whom faced intense persecution for their faith.

The issues that Paul addressed in his letters to the first-century church are no less important to today's believers. Paul laid a very practical foundation for *how* to live the Christian life, even in the face of struggles, temptations, and false teachings. His personal example of seeking to know and obey Christ Jesus, no matter what the cost, remains an example to all who call themselves Christians. "I in Christ and Christ in me" was Paul's unwavering theme song.

AN OVERVIEW OF OUR STUDY
OF THE EPISTLE OF GALATIANS

This study guide presents seven lessons drawn from and based largely upon the Epistle of Galatians. The study guide elaborates and is developed around the commentary included in the Blackaby Study Bible:

Lesson #1: Only One Gospel

Lesson #2: Justified by Faith

Lesson #3: Children and Heirs

Lesson #4: The Works of the Flesh

Lesson #5: The Fruit of the Spirit

Lesson #6: Bearing Burdens and Loads

Lesson #7: Sowing and Reaping

Personal or Group Use. These lessons are offered for personal study and reflection, or for small-group Bible study. The questions asked may be answered by an individual reader, or used as a foundation for group discussion. A segment titled "Notes to Leaders of Small Groups" is included at the back of this book to help those who might lead a group study of the material here.

Before you embark on this study, we encourage you to read in full the statement in the *Blackaby Study Bible* titled "How to Study the Bible." Our contention is always that the Bible is unique among all literature. It is God's definitive word for humanity. The Bible is:

- *inspired*—"God breathed"

- *authoritative*—absolutely the "final word" on any spiritual matter

- *the plumb line of truth*—the standard against which all human activity and reasoning must be evaluated

The Bible is fascinating in that it has remarkable diversity, but also remarkable unity. The books were penned by an eclectic assortment of authors representing a variety of languages and cultures. The Bible as a whole has a number of literary forms. But, the Bible's message from cover to cover is clear, consistent, and unified.

More than mere words on a page, the Bible is an encounter with God Himself. No book is more critical to your life. The very essence of the Bible is the Lord Himself, Jesus Christ.

God speaks by the Holy Spirit through the Bible. He also communicates during your time of prayer, in your life circumstances, and through the church. Read your Bible in an attitude of prayer, and allow the Holy Spirit to make you aware of God's activity in your personal life. Write down what you learn, meditate on it, and adjust your thoughts, attitudes, and behavior accordingly. Look for ways every day in which the truth of God's Word can be applied to your circumstances and relationships. God is not random, but orderly and intentional in the way He speaks to you.

Be encouraged—the Bible is *not* too difficult for the average person to understand if that person asks the Holy Spirit for help. (Furthermore, not even the most brilliant person can fully understand the Bible apart from the Holy Spirit's help!) God desires for you to know Him and to know His Word. Every person who reads the Bible can learn from it. The person who will receive *maximum* benefit from reading and studying the Bible, however, is the person who:

- *is born again* (John 3:3, 5). Those who are born again and have received the gift of His Spirit have a distinct advantage in understanding the deeper truths of God's Word.

- *has a heart that desires to learn God's truth.* Your attitude influences greatly the outcome of Bible study. Resist the temptation to focus on what others have said about the Bible. Allow the Holy Spirit to guide you as you study God's Word for yourself.

- *has a heart that seeks to obey God.* The Holy Spirit teaches those who desire to apply what they learn.

Begin your Bible study with prayer, asking the Holy Spirit to guide your thoughts and to impress upon you what is on God's heart. Then, make plans to adjust your life immediately to obey the Lord fully.

As you read and study the Bible, your purpose is not to *create* meaning, but to *discover* the meaning of the text with the Holy Spirit's guidance. Ask yourself, "What did the author have in mind? How was this applied by those who first heard these words?" Especially in your study of the Gospel accounts, pay attention to the words of Jesus that begin "truly, truly" or "He opened His mouth and taught them, saying...." These are core principles and teachings that have powerful impact on *every* person's life.

At times you may find it helpful to consult other passages of the Bible (made available in the center columns in the Blackaby Study Bible), or the commentary that is in the margins of the Blackaby Study Bible.

Keep in mind always that Bible study is not primarily an exercise for acquiring information, but an opportunity for transformation. Bible study is your opportunity to encounter God and to be changed in His presence. When God speaks to your heart, nothing remains the same. Jesus said, "He who has ears to hear, let him hear" (Matt. 13:9). Choose to have ears that desire to hear!

The B-A-S-I-Cs of Each Study in This Guide. Each lesson in this study guide has five segments, using the word BASIC as an acronym. The word BASIC does not allude to elementary or "simple," but rather, to "foundational." These studies extend the concepts that are part of the Blackaby Study Bible commentary and are focused on key aspects of what it means to be a Christ-follower in today's world. The BASIC acronym stands for:

B = *Bible Focus*. This segment presents the central passage for the lesson and a general explanation that covers the central theme or concern.

A = *Application for Today*. This segment has a story or illustration related to modern-day times, with questions that link the Bible text to today's issues, problems, and concerns.

S = *Supplementary Scriptures to Consider*. In this segment, other Bible verses related to the general theme of the lesson are explored.

I = *Introspection and Implications*. In this segment, questions are asked that lead to deeper reflection about one's personal faith journey and life experiences.

C = *Communicating the Good News*. In this segment, challenging questions are aimed at ways in which the truth of the lesson might be lived out and shared with others (either to win the lost or build up the church).

LESSON #1
ONLY ONE GOSPEL

Gospel: good news—and specifically the Good News about Jesus Christ

B
Bible Focus

> *I marvel that you are turning away so soon from Him who called you in the grace of Christ, to a different gospel, which is not another; but there are some who trouble you and want to pervert the gospel of Christ. But even if we, or an angel from heaven, preach any other gospel to you than what we have preached to you, let him be accursed. As we have said before, so now I say again, if anyone preaches any other gospel to you than what you have received, let him be accursed . . .*
>
> *But I make known to you, brethren, that the gospel which was preached by me is not according to man. For I neither received it from man, nor was I taught it, but it came through the revelation of Jesus Christ (Galatians 1:6–9, 11–12).*

Human nature is fickle. Any person who has ever ridden the waves of fame knows that. Popularity rises and falls. Emotions run hot and cold. Styles come and go. Fads are "in" today and "out" tomorrow. Political parties expand and contract. The stock market rises and falls, often reflecting an ebb and flow of societal opinion and intuition. Human philosophies gain in strength, and then wane. Methods change. Protocols are updated. Technology advances.

Against the fluctuations of human nature and invention stands the unchanging nature of God. As the New Testament states simply and eloquently, "Jesus Christ is the same yesterday, today, and forever" (Hebrews 13:8).

The apostle Paul had preached to the people of Galatia a message of free grace: nothing that a person could do earns the love of God—a person can only fling himself on God's mercy in an act of faith. When a person does so, God responds out of His unchanging nature of love and forgives, reconciles, and redeems.

Salvation is not about what man does. It is about what Christ Jesus has already accomplished.

Salvation is not about ways in which man might achieve worthiness. It is about God declaring that salvation is available to all who will believe and receive. John 3:16 tells us plainly, "whoever believes in Him should not perish but have everlasting life."

Salvation is not about achievement. It is about acceptance.

Salvation is not rooted in religious practice. It is rooted in relationship with God.

Shortly after the Galatians had heard and received Paul's message, Jewish Christians arrived on the scene and taught that *in addition to* believing in Jesus, the new Gentile converts needed to follow Jewish laws, including the ritual of circumcision, in order to fully please God. They taught further that, every time a new convert performed a deed of the law, he received a "credit entry" on God's ledger, all of which added up to reward. It is this teaching that Paul came against as a valiant warrior wielding a powerful spiritual sword.

"No!" Paul declared to the Galatians. "God showed me directly and personally by my own salvation that there is nothing about keeping the law that produces salvation." Paul, of course, had been fanatical about keeping the law. As a Pharisee, he prided himself in law-keeping and had been an arch-enemy of the early church. If keeping the law could have produced salvation in any person, it would have been Paul. "But that didn't happen," Paul taught. "Jesus made it very clear to me on the road to Damascus that 'accepting Him' as Savior was all that was required for a dramatic change in one's spiritual nature."

Countless people around the world today are in bondage to a long list of "must do's," which they believe are a ladder to God's favor. Some cut themselves, others travel miles on bloody knees, still others engage in a series of good works to earn enough points to be fully accepted into what they believe will be the next level of piety.

Even within Christian denominations, we find certain rituals and codes of dress, speech, and behavior "required" for a person to be fully accepted spiritually.

Why?

Perhaps the ultimate answer is human pride. As human beings, we believe that there must be *something* that we can do, must do, or "get to do" in order to achieve forgiveness and reconciliation with God. We want to have a part, to feel as if we in some way "deserve" God's reception of us.

The truth of the Gospel, however, is that nothing more is required for salvation—only believing and receiving, an opening of one's life to say yes to God.

Are you willing to make it that simple for a person to accept Jesus as Savior?

We tend to regard simple things as being simplistic and of less value. There is nothing simplistic about the Gospel, however, and nothing easy— perhaps the most *difficult* thing that a person can do is push his own pride out of the way and admit that he needs the love of God and can do nothing to earn it.

A
Application for Today

The little boy crumpled up the piece of paper and threw it on the floor. It joined at least a dozen other crumpled up balls of paper.

"What are you working on?" the boy's mother asked as she entered his room, saw her son sitting at his desk, and saw the pile of paper growing around his feet.

"I'm trying to draw a picture for God," he said.

"What are you drawing?" Mother asked, unfolding and smoothing one of the discarded pieces of paper.

"You and Dad and me and Jane," he said.

"Looks like Buffy the dog is here, too," Mom said. "So why have you thrown away your work?" she added, smoothing out a second drawing.

"None of them are good enough for God," the boy said. "I'm a bad artist. I can't get it right."

The mother pulled her son close. "I feel certain that God would like any of these drawings that you have done," she said. "They come from your heart. But what you draw for God isn't nearly as valuable to Him as *you* are. He loves you, regardless of your art skills."

"I know," the boy nodded as his mother held him close. "But I wanted to give Him something great."

"Give him your heart," Mom said. "That's the greatest gift you can give. And you know what?"

"What?" the boy asked.

"When you give God your heart, He gives you His."

Do you struggle today thinking that you have to *do* something in order to win God's approval? His love? His forgiveness?

Do you struggle with feelings that you are unworthy of God's love?

What is it that God really wants?

S
Supplementary Scriptures to Consider

Paul noted that the Galatians had been freed from pagan rituals when they came to Christ, but had then resorted to religious rituals. In essence, they had turned from one list of things to do to another list of things required. Paul wrote:

> When you did not know God, you served those which by
> nature are not gods. But now after you have known God, or

rather are known by God, how is it that you turn again to the
weak and beggarly elements, to which you desire again to be
in bondage? You observe days and months and seasons and
years. I am afraid for you, lest I have labored for you in vain
(Galatians 4:8–11).

• Were there certain protocols that you followed or rituals that you kept
  before you became a Christian, hoping that these deeds would make you
  "good enough" for God?

• Are there things that you do today with a secret hope or belief that these
  things will keep you from losing your salvation? Is there anything that
  you don't dare "stop" because you fear that God will be so angry with
  you that He will cast you away?

• Are there certain rituals that you believe you must follow in order to
  retain God's favor and protection? How did you develop these beliefs?
  Did they come from God or your own thinking?

• What do you believe the apostle Paul would say to you if you answered yes to any of the above questions?

Paul told the Galatians that the false teachers were attempting to influence them, not for their good but in order to cause division in the church. The false teachers sought to exclude those who didn't follow their teachings and to create personal fan clubs among those who did. Paul wrote:

> They [the false teachers] zealously court you, but for no good; yes, they want to exclude you, that you may be zealous for them. But it is good to be zealous in a good thing always, and not only when I am present with you. My little children, for whom I labor in birth again unto Christ is formed in you. I would like to be present with you now and to change my tone; for I have doubts about you (Galatians 4:17–20).

• Are you aware of a situation where religious rituals took precedence over relationships and caused division among God's people? How do you think God felt when His children were hurt?

Paul had experienced both spiritual bondage to the law, and spiritual freedom in Christ:

> Stand fast therefore in the liberty by which Christ has made us free, and do not be entangled again with a yoke of bondage. . . .

> For in Christ Jesus neither circumcision nor uncircumcision
> avails anything but faith working through love (Galatians 5:1, 6).

• Why do you believe some people who have experienced spiritual freedom
in Christ might be tempted to return to rituals, practices, or beliefs that
kept them in spiritual bondage?

• What does the phrase "faith working through love" mean to you?

• In what ways does the love of God free us to do what God desires, rather
than what mankind requires?

Paul focused on the motive for those who were teaching that the Gentile
converts needed to be circumcised—they were seeking to elevate themselves
as spiritual authorities and to exert power:

> For not even those who are circumcised keep the law, but they
> desire to have you circumcised that they may boast in your

flesh. But God forbid that I should boast except in the cross of our Lord Jesus Christ, by whom the world has been crucified to me, and I to the world. For in Christ Jesus neither circumcision nor uncircumcision avails anything, but a new creation (Galatians 6:13–15).

- Are there any religious rituals that you believe can *create* a "newness" of spiritual life?

- Most rites and rituals within the Christian faith are called an "outward and visible sign of an inward and invisible reality." They function as a witness—both to the person participating in the ritual and to those who are observing it—that a spiritual transformation has taken or is taking place. Have you ever participated in a ritual that you believe was *reflective* of a change in your inner being?

- Have you ever participated in a religious ritual or practice that had no personal meaning for you? How did you feel? What were the ongoing results?

I
Introspection and Implications

1. To what extent are we creatures of habit? Does this work for us, or against us, as we come to Christ, accept Him as Savior, and then seek to follow Him as our Lord?

2. We live in a society that places high value on achievement as a means of acquiring status. What challenges have you faced in your Christian walk when it comes to feelings of worthiness? Do you see yourself as being a successful Christian? Why or why not? How does your definition of success relate to God's definitions of success?

3. Most people label themselves as "overachiever," "underachiever," or "average." Why are these labels inappropriate when it comes to salvation? How are these labels counterproductive to our ongoing spiritual growth?

C
Communicating the Good News

What must a person *do* to experience God's free gift of salvation?

What must a new convert *do* to be fully acceptable to God?

What must we *do* to grow spiritually? What scripture would you use to support your answer?

LESSON #2

JUSTIFIED BY FAITH

Justification: to be forgiven of sin and put into right relationship with God

B
Bible Focus

> When Peter had come to Antioch, I withstood him to his
> face, because he was to be blamed; for before certain men
> came from James, he would eat with the Gentiles; but when
> they came, he withdrew and separated himself, fearing those
> who were of the circumcision. And the rest of the Jews also
> played the hypocrite with him, so that even Barnabas was
> carried away with their hypocrisy.
>
> But when I saw that they were not straightforward about the
> truth of the gospel, I said to Peter before them all, "If you,
> being a Jew, live in the manner of Gentiles and not as the Jews,
> why do you compel Gentiles to live as Jews? We who are Jews
> by nature, and not sinners of the Gentiles, knowing that a man
> is not justified by the works of the law, but by faith in Jesus
> Christ, even we have believed in Christ Jesus, that we might be
> justified by faith in Christ and not by the works of the law; for
> by the works of the law no flesh shall be justified . . .
>
> For I through the law died to the law that I might live to
> God. I have been crucified with Christ; it is no longer I who
> live, but Christ lives in me; and the life which I now live in the
> flesh I live by faith in the Son of God, who loved me and gave
> Himself for me. I do not set aside the grace of God; for if
> righteousness comes through the law, then Christ died in
> vain" (Galatians 2:11–16, 19–21).

Many people have a strong desire to fit in with others around them. Peer
pressure is not limited to teenagers or young people. People of all ages and
in all strata of society desire the approval of others. The believers in Antioch
were no different. They were adapting their behavior to fit in—keeping the
customs and rituals of Judaism when they were with Jewish Christians, and
keeping the customs and rituals of the Gentile believers when they were with
them.

Paul labeled their hypocrisy for what it was. The Jews had been saved by
faith, not by keeping the law. Their means of salvation was the same as that
of the Gentiles. To resort to law-keeping was to create two different classes
of Christians.

The word "hypocrisy" was well known to the Gentiles of Galatia. Greek
theater made extensive use of masks. One actor might play several roles by
means of different masks. The word hypocrisy relates directly to one face
wearing two or more masks. The happy face of comedy and the sad face of

tragedy came out of this theatrical device. Paul clearly taught the believers in Galatia that the wearing of spiritual masks was not warranted in Christ. Our integrity as Christians rests in our being the same person regardless of circumstances or settings.

Christianity does not allow any separate-but-equal paths when it comes to salvation, forgiveness of sins, and the gift of eternal life. There is only one path—the one that leads directly to the cross and the acknowledgment that Jesus' death on the cross was the definitive, substitutionary, atoning sacrifice for sin. What Jesus accomplished on the cross has been made available to all mankind for the remission of sin. Nothing else is required, and nothing else can substitute or compete with the final work of the shed blood of Christ Jesus on the cross.

Do you ever find yourself adapting your language or behavior to "accommodate" the beliefs of others who are not Christians? Perhaps at work? Perhaps in a social setting?

Do you ever find yourself cringing at the possibility that you may have to defend your belief in Christ Jesus as being the *only* means of salvation, forgiveness of sin, and a transformed life?

Do you ever find yourself searching for ways of accommodating the customs or rituals of people who visit your home or become members of a social club to which you belong?

Do you ever find yourself "shutting down" and refusing to fully engage in conversation with a family member who is opposed to Christ and critical of your relationship with Christ?

Every person faces challenges when it comes to maintaining integrity and refusing to fall into hypocrisy. How do you handle those challenges? What do you do if you feel that you have been hypocritical?

To what extent is it acceptable to adapt to others and still maintain a strong witness for Christ?

A
Application for Today

As the thirteen-year-old climbed into the family van, she immediately burst into tears. "What's wrong?" her parents asked in unison.

"Just drive, please," their daughter pleaded. "Let's get out of here."

Dad complied, but two blocks away, he pulled into the parking lot of a neighborhood park. "What happened?" he asked.

"I wish I hadn't gone to that stupid party," the girl said.

"But why? You were looking forward to this," her mother said.

"Nobody told me I had to wear a dress," the girl said.

"A dress?" her mother asked. "It was an outdoor picnic, wasn't it?"

"Yes!" the girl said. "But Frank's mother is very old-fashioned and she doesn't believe that girls should wear makeup or cut their hair or wear pants of any kind. She doesn't even believe that girls should wear tops that have short sleeves. And here I show up in jeans and a sleeveless t-shirt. She made me put on one of her old sweaters!"

"You're kidding," her mother whispered to herself.

"I've heard of church people who have very strict dress codes," Dad said, "but I didn't know Frank's parents were like that."

"And that isn't all," their daughter added. "I overheard Frank's mother say to him, 'I thought you told me that all of the young people you invited were Christians. Some of them apparently don't live what they profess to believe . . . a couple of your young female friends don't know that truly saved people dress modestly, and not like men. I wonder if they are really saved.' I nearly died of embarrassment. I felt like I was in ancient history. And who is she, anyway, to question whether I'm saved?"

Later that evening Mom and Dad had a discussion of their own. They recalled the days, not many years ago, when all of the children and teens at the Christian school where they had sent their children were required to wear dresses to school—no bra straps showing and no bare midriffs allowed. They recalled the time when they had been teenagers, and had attended churches that frowned on Christians going to movies, much less dancing.

"Are we more right today than our parents and grandparents?" Mom asked.

"To what degree do works go hand-in-hand with faith?" Dad asked. What do *you* say?

Even if works do not produce salvation, is there a degree to which works *reflect* salvation? If salvation is not justified by works, is a person's *witness* still in some way justified by works? Why or why not?

S
Supplementary Scriptures to Consider

Paul also wrote this to the Galatians:

> O foolish Galatians! Who has bewitched you that you should not obey the truth. . . . He who supplies the Spirit to you and works miracles among you, does He do it by the works of the law, or by the hearing of faith?—just as Abraham "believed God, and it was accounted to him for righteousness." There-

fore, know that only those who are of faith are sons of Abraham. And the Scripture, foreseeing that God would justify the
Gentiles by faith, preached the gospel to Abraham beforehand,
saying, "'In you all the nations shall be blessed.'" So then,
those who are of faith are blessed with believing Abraham
(Galatians 3:1, 5–9).

• To be "bewitched" means to be "deceived." Have you ever been deceived
  by someone who convinced you that certain works were necessary for
  salvation? How did you come to recognize the truth?

• Do you believe that there are any human works that must be added to the
  work of the Holy Spirit for your salvation to be secure or ensured?

Paul showed the Galatians that the law was a curse, because no person can
ever fully do everything that God commands. There is no way that any
human being can obey all of the Law in all ways at all times. Paul wrote:

Christ has redeemed us from the curse of the law, having
become a curse for us (for it is written, "Cursed is everyone
who hangs on a tree"), that the blessing of Abraham might
come upon the Gentiles in Christ Jesus, that we might receive
the promise of the Spirit through faith (Galatians 3:13–14).

- In your past, can you cite specific ways in which you felt that you were a "failure" at keeping God's commandments? Did you continue in these feelings or allow God to forgive and restore you?

- To what extent must we *believe* the promise of the Spirit's help before we see evidence of His help in our lives?

Paul knew that tutors played an important role in Greek and Roman households. Wealthy parents hired tutors to instruct, protect, and correct their young children, just as a nanny might be hired today. Tutors were known for being demanding more than being loving. Paul wrote:

> The law was our tutor to bring us to Christ, that we might be justified by faith. But after faith has come, we are no longer under a tutor (Galatians 3:24–25).

- What does the law teach you about God? About the sinful nature of unredeemed mankind?

- How does the law reveal a *need* for salvation?

- Paul noted that, after a person had put his trust in Christ Jesus, the law was no longer a tutor. Rather, the Holy Spirit—whom Jesus called the Spirit of Truth and the Helper (John 14:10)—instructs, protects, and corrects the believer. How have you experienced instruction by the Holy Spirit? Correction? Protection?

I

Introspection and Implications

1. Is there any person's opinion that counts as much to you as the opinion of God?

2. To what degree do you believe it is important to be "your authentic self" in every situation and circumstance? Are there ever any situations in which adaptation to another person's belief system or values is warranted or prudent? Why or why not?

3. Have you ever "changed" denominations—perhaps you grew up in one Christian denomination and then, as an adult, transferred your membership to another Christian denomination? What "cultural" differences did you encounter? Were additional rules placed upon you? How did you respond? (Were "fewer" rules placed upon you? If so, how did you respond?)

4. What is the difference between "keeping religious rules" and "building relationship with Christ"?

5. How do you live in the "freedom of Christ" within your church and denominational setting? Does there have to be any "tension" between the two?

6. In what ways can membership in a church strengthen, encourage, and protect your relationship with God?

C
Communicating the Good News

In what ways are we wise to guard at all times against placing an emphasis on man-made religious rules as we present the Gospel to an unsaved person?

Why is it important to place emphasis on relationship with Christ Jesus rather than religion in presenting the Gospel?

LESSON #3

CHILDREN AND HEIRS

Heir: one who by right or by law receives the property, position, or title of another person when that person dies

B
Bible Focus

> *You are all sons of God through faith in Christ Jesus. For as many of you as were baptized into Christ have put on Christ. There is neither Jew nor Greek, there is neither slave nor free, there is neither male nor female; for you are all one in Christ Jesus. And if you are Christ's, then you are Abraham's seed, and heirs according to the promise . . .*
>
> *And because you are sons, God has sent forth the Spirit of His Son into your hearts, crying out, "Abba, Father!" Therefore you are no longer a slave but a son, and if a son, then an heir of God through Christ (Galatians 3:26–29, 4:6–7).*

The Kingdom of God is much bigger than any one Christian denomination. It spans all denominations and all nations to include *all* who place their faith in Jesus as Savior, and who seek to follow Him as their Lord. In many ways the Kingdom, and its local expression in the church, is our extended family, most certainly a fully "blended" family of many cultures, races, nationalities, ages, and socioeconomic strata.

The Gospel and the letters of Paul agree fully that all who accept Jesus as Savior are equal before God when it comes to being members of God's family. We are heirs with Christ Jesus of the fullness of God's spiritual riches. God does not withhold any of His blessings to His children on the basis of their human nature, levels of achievement, or cultural background. Rather, He blesses His children with equal access to Him through prayer, with an equal promise of the Holy Spirit to indwell, counsel, guide, and help; and with an equal opportunity to grow into spiritual maturity and manifest fully the character and likeness of Christ Jesus. All spiritual gifts and rewards are made available to the Christian who will pursue Him by faith.

Why then are there so many difficulties within the church?

We are not all alike. We do not lose any of our talents, abilities, intelligence, emotional temperament, or developed skills when we accept Jesus as Savior Each member of the body is uniquely gifted to build up the entire church.

We also retain our free will to choose God's presence and power in our lives, or to reject the opportunities that God makes available to us. We are not robots. Furthermore, we do not lose our basic personality—our quirks, creative bent, and distinctive traits. The person that God made in creation is now filled with His Spirit to do His will.

Our uniqueness remains, and this ultimately is for the benefit of the church as a whole, and for us as individuals. It is our individuality that qualifies us to fulfill our niche in any given society and in the church—our unique blend of gifts, talents, and personality make us supremely suited for a particular God-designed role and purpose. God ensures in this way that all jobs that need to be accomplished are accomplished, and that all gifts function within a church for the good of the whole.

What makes a strong family? When siblings recognize clearly their commonalities in having the same heritage, and also honor their distinctive differences as individuals. What makes a strong church? When believers acknowledge their common faith, and enter into a giving and receiving relationship with others, when it comes to the function of their life empowered by the Holy Spirit.

What weakens a family? When siblings regard one another as rivals, never fully believing that the parents love each child equally. What weakens a church? When members begin to compete against one another, striving to gain more spiritual power or influence.

Do you acknowledge that those who are Christians in other denominations are equal heirs with you before God?

Why or why not?

Do you *like* your brothers and sisters in Christ? Including those from other denominations?

Why or why not?

How might your feelings of spiritual "sibling rivalry" be set aside?

A
Application for Today

Three siblings were at odds after the death of Dad. Mom had gone to be with the Lord years earlier, and for various reasons, only one of the siblings had been a steady caregiver for Dad in the intervening years. That sibling believed that he should have a greater stake in the inheritance that Dad had left to the three of them. The other two, as might be expected, disagreed.

At issue, especially, was the disposition of the family farm. One sibling wanted to run the farm and receive half of the income from it, dividing the other half between his siblings. One sibling wanted to lease out the farm and share equally in the "rent." One sibling wanted to sell the farm and divide the proceeds three ways.

And then things became particularly difficult. A *fourth* person showed up, with photographs and letters that indicated that she, too, was a child of Dad. She had been conceived before Dad came to Christ Jesus, before he had married Mom, and before any of the other three siblings had been born. Without the other three siblings knowing of her existence, Dad—and Mom, when she was alive—had maintained a distant but fairly consistent relationship with this "elder sister." Since Dad's last will and testament did not designate heirs by name, it appeared to the three siblings that they now had to entertain a fourth opinion in what to do with the family farm.

If you are in a discussion group faced with this scenario, the opinions in your group are likely to differ as much as the opinions of these four siblings differed! At the heart of the matter is the question: What does it really mean to be an *heir*?

Apply this situation to your local church. How do you feel about those who are on your church's membership roles, but who rarely attend? How do you feel about those who seem to "come from afar" and lay claim to full participation in your church? How do you feel when newcomers move into leadership roles?

Are there any blessings that you believe the Lord reserves for those who are more mature believers or more longstanding faithful church members? Why or why not?

To what degree do you believe that ALL believers in Christ Jesus are equal heirs of God?

S
Supplementary Scriptures to Consider

Paul clearly recognized that all *believers* are sons of God, but not all *people* are heirs of God. Paul referred to Isaac, the son of Sarah and Abraham, as the Hebrew child of promise. The bondwoman and her son were Hagar and Ishmael. Isaac was the father of Jacob, and the grandfather of the twelve tribes of Israel. Ishmael was sent from the home of Sarah and Abraham, as was allowable under the rules regarding servants and their masters. Paul had this in mind when he wrote:

> Now we, brethren, as Isaac was, are children of promise. But as he who was born according to the flesh then persecuted him who was born according to the Spirit, even so it is now. Nevertheless what does the Scripture say? "Cast out the bondwoman and her son, for the son of the bondwoman shall not be heir with the son of the freewoman." So then, brethren, we are not children of the bondswoman but of the free (Galatians 4:28–31).

- We live in a democratic nation where all people are considered equal in matters of law, regardless of their religious affiliations. Why is it difficult to accept the message of the New Testament that not all people are "equal" when it comes to receiving God's blessings?

• How would you reply to a person who said to you, "Every person on the earth is a child of God"? How do the concepts "beloved child" and "created being" differ?

• What truly makes a person a *child* of God?

Paul addressed a question that concerns many Christians—how do I know that I am a child of God and joint heir with Christ?

> For you did not receive the spirit of bondage again to fear, but you received the Spirit of adoption by whom we cry out, "Abba, Father." The Spirit Himself bears witness with our spirit that we are children of God, and if children, then heirs— heirs of God and joint heirs with Christ, if needed we suffer with Him, that we may also be glorified together (Romans 8:12–17).

• What does the phrase "Spirit of adoption" mean to you? Does this refer to how you *feel*, or to the truth of what the Holy Spirit has done in you when you accepted Jesus as your Savior?

Paul recognized that children and slaves were often treated alike in Greek and Roman households—both were subject to discipline, daily direction, and confinement or restraints. The difference lay in the fact that when a *child* reached adulthood, he was given freedom to make his own choices, and to pursue his own destiny. Paul wrote to the Galatians:

> Now I say that the heir, as long as he is a child, does not differ at all from a slave, though he is master of all, but is under guardians and stewards until the time appointed by the father. Even so we, when we were children, were in bondage under the elements of the world. But when the fullness of the time had come, God sent forth His Son, born of a woman, born under the law, to redeem those who were under the law, that we might receive the adoption as sons (Galatians 4:1–5).

• Those who are in "bondage under the elements of the world" are subject to being ruled by their own natural instincts, which dictate decisions and choices as environments and circumstances change. Those who are saved have been given an ongoing choice to ask the Holy Spirit to guide their steps and lead them to a purposeful and fulfilled destiny, and have been given the ability to obey the Spirit and over-rule their own fleshly instincts. In what ways have you experienced this in your life?

- Did you perhaps once "go with the flow" and do whatever "felt good" to you? Do you now experience greater restraint?

- In what ways has becoming a Christian led you to become a more responsible person?

I

Introspection and Implications

1. How do you personally respond to the concept of large family as it is applied to the church? Are you comfortable being part of a greater family of God or do you prefer to see your spiritual relationship with God to be that of an only child?

2. What obligations do you have for family members that you do not have for people who are not in your family? How does this apply to the church? Do you have feelings of responsibility or obligation toward

those who are fellow believers that you do not have for those who are outside the church?

3. Why is it difficult to regard people who are different as being "equal" before God?

4. Jesus clearly taught that people have differing degrees of talents and abilities. In what ways is it difficult not to see those with greater talents as being more "special" to God?

5. Cite specific ways in which all believers are equal before God.

6. How receptive are the members of your church to newcomers who might be of a different race, ethnicity, culture, or nationality?

C
Communicating the Good News

Unbelievers often feel unworthy of God's love and forgiveness. In what practical ways might we convey the truth that God offers salvation to *all*, not on the basis of merits in the person, but on the basis of His own unchanging love and mercy?

LESSON #4

THE WORKS OF THE FLESH

Flesh: the physical body and all natural instincts that arise from physical needs and drives
Lust: a very strong desire to obtain satisfaction for a physical or emotional drive

B
Bible Focus

> *I say then: Walk in the Spirit, and you shall not full the lust
> of the flesh. For the flesh lusts against the Spirit, and the Spirit
> against the flesh; and these are contrary to one another, so
> that you do not do the things that you wish. But if you are led
> by the Spirit, you are not under the law.*
>
> *Now the works of the flesh are evident, which are: adultery,
> fornication, uncleanness, lewdness, idolatry, sorcery, hatred,
> contentions, jealousies, outbursts of wrath, selfish ambitions,
> dissensions, heresies, envy, murders, drunkenness, revelries,
> and the like; of which I tell you beforehand, just as I also told
> you in time past, that those who practice such things will not
> inherit the kingdom of God (Galatians 5:16–21).*

Perhaps more than any other author of the New Testament, the apostle
Paul preached and taught freedom in Christ Jesus. He wrote consistently
about a person's freedom to choose Christ as Savior, freedom to pursue a
godly life, freedom to seek and develop spiritual maturity, and freedom in
having access to all that the Holy Spirit offered to the believer. The freedom
of the Christian, however, was never freedom to do as one pleases.

Freedom in Christ is freedom *from* sin, not freedom *to* sin. Freedom in
Christ is freedom to *choose* a godly way of life—the believer has been set
free from the bondage of old habits and old instincts that once compelled the
person to sin virtually without thought and without an ability to stop sinning.

Paul listed a number of behaviors as "works of the flesh." These are
behaviors that seem acceptable to the unbeliever, but should never be regarded as acceptable to the believer. "Acceptability" is perhaps the easiest
demarcation between flesh and Spirit in the writings of Paul. Those who live
by the flesh or have a fleshly nature regard sin as doing what comes natu-
rally, instinctively. The behaviors are deemed "acceptable" expressions of
humanity. Those who live by the Spirit, in contrast, consider it unacceptable
to do anything that is contrary to God's commandments or God's greater
purposes in the person's life, regardless of feelings or the intensity of a
human drive.

The works identified by Paul are something of a catalog of evil deeds, but
this list is by no means a definitive or complete definition of evil. Rather, the
list indicates that there are behaviors that *should* be considered unacceptable
to a believer, regardless of race, cultural tradition, or nationality:

- adultery and fornication—having sex with any person who is not your spouse (whether married or unmarried)

- uncleanness or impurity—the word in the Greek language has been used to refer to unpruned trees, unclean and festering wounds, or materials that have not had impurities sifted from them. The overall sense is of things that are unsuitable to a fruitful, healthy, useful life. In the spiritual sense, impurity is anything that soils a person's relationship with God.

- lewdness—being preoccupied in seeking sexual pleasure

- idolatry—worship of material objects in place of God

- sorcery—literally the "use of drugs" that were a part of witchcraft in Paul's time

- hatred—enmity, hostility toward others

- contentions— strife, rivalry that results in wrangling and quarreling

- jealousies—envy, a desire to have what is not rightfully one's property or relationship

- outbursts of wrath—uncontrolled anger, bursts of temper

- selfish ambitions—those who seek personal power, fame, or wealth so they can fulfill their own desires, without regard to the welfare or honor of others

- dissensions—the word in Greek means literally "to stand apart," to create division by refusing to come together with others for the good of all

- heresies—holding to beliefs or values that are not godly

- envy—not only wanting what others have, but seeking to take from others what one wants

- murders—killing to advance self (including the killing of reputation, killing of relationship)

- drunkenness—too much alcohol

- revelries—unrestrained carousing that can quickly turn into rioting or unrighteous behavior on the part of individuals or groups

It is interesting to note that those things which Paul regarded as inherently ungodly behaviors are *still* considered by the vast majority of people in our society today to be ungodly behavior. Human nature has not changed. Those who find such behaviors acceptable live in a way that is contrary to the Spirit.

How difficult is it for a Christian to give up the works of the flesh?

Has it been difficult for you?

A
Application for Today

"What happens if I mess up?" the man asked his spiritual mentor after reading the above passage from the Epistle to the Galatians.

"Ask God for forgiveness," the mentor replied.

The man sighed deeply. "Every time? Will God forgive me even if I mess up more than once?"

"God forgives every time we come to Him with a genuinely repentant heart," the mentor replied.

The man asked, "What do you mean, a 'genuinely repentant heart'? Does that mean 'I'm sorry'?"

The mentor replied, "The bigger question when you 'mess up,' as you say, is to ask yourself, 'do I *want* to keep messing up from time to time?' If the answer is 'yes,' you aren't truly desiring to walk in the Spirit. You enjoy walking in the flesh and, although you may not indulge in a particular sin as a habit, or even frequently, you want to have that sin as an option on those occasions when you *do* want to sin. If the answer is 'no, I don't want to keep messing up,' you are genuinely repentant and want the Holy Spirit to help you make a change in the way that you respond to your own perceptions, human drives, and impulses."

The man was reflective and silent. His mentor added, "Note that Paul said we are to 'walk in the Spirit.' Even believers sometimes fall down as they walk down the dirty paths of this life, but at issue is whether they choose to stay down and wallow in the muddy pathway, or get up, be cleansed, and walk on with greater awareness of the path and greater reliance upon the Spirit. Paul also said to be 'led by the Spirit.' The Spirit will not lead us to fall. He helps us get up and makes us more aware of the path that we walk and our need to stay reliant upon Him for guidance."

What about you?

Are you assured that God forgives those who commit "works of the flesh"?

Are you seeking to "walk in the Spirit"?

Do you desire to be led by the Spirit and refrain from all works of the flesh?

S
Supplementary Scriptures to Consider

Paul concluded his discourse on walking in the Spirit by writing:

> Let us not become conceited, provoking one another, envying one another (Galatians 5:26).

- In what ways are the works of the flesh reflective of
  CONCEIT?
  PROVOKING (COMPETING WITH) ONE ANOTHER?
  ENVY?

The works of the flesh that Paul cited all lead to some degree of division among believers. Paul wrote:

> For you, brethren, have been called to liberty; only do not use liberty as an opportunity for the flesh, but through love serve one another. For all the law is fulfilled in one word, even in this: "You shall love your neighbor as yourself" (Galatians 5:13–15).

- How do the works of the flesh in Galatians 5:19–21 tear away at the fabric of the church, or relationships between believers in Christ? Consider them one by one:

Adultery and Fornication —

Impurity —

Lewdness —

Idolatry —

Sorcery —

Hatred —

Contentions —

Jealousies —

Outbursts of Wrath —

Selfish Ambitions —

Dissensions —

Heresies —

Envy —

Murders —

Drunkenness —

Revelries —

- Is it ever acceptable to engage in just a "little bit" of a work of the flesh? Why or why not?

• What does it mean to you to "serve one another" in love?

• In what ways does love and a desire to serve others keep us from engaging in the works of the flesh?

I
Introspection and Implications

1. Paul warned the Galatians not to "practice" the works of the flesh. What difference do you see between an error in judgment and developing a *habit* that reflects ongoing fleshly living?

2. Paul said that those who practice the works of the flesh "will not inherit the kingdom of God"? What does this mean to you? What difference do you see between the gift of eternal life and "inheriting the kingdom of God"?

3. How important is it that a person's "lifestyle" reflect change after that person comes to Christ? Is this the work of the individual believer's will, the influence of the church, or the compelling work of the Holy Spirit in the believer's life?

4. What does it mean to you to "walk in the Spirit"?

5. What does it mean to you to be "led by the Spirit"?

C
Communicating the Good News

In what ways might an unbeliever consider it difficult or impossible to give up a pattern of sin? What assurance can you give an unbeliever that the Holy Spirit will help him or her turn from sin to godly living?

Do you believe that people truly enjoy "works of the flesh" over time, and as habits?

How important is it to reach people with the Gospel message when they "hit bottom" and find their own behavior to be a heavy burden or something that they desire to change?

How important is it to teach our children to trust the Holy Spirit to lead them so they might not fall victim to the ravages of the "works of the flesh"?

Lesson #5

THE FRUIT OF THE SPIRIT

Fruit: the production of something worthwhile, or beneficial for consumption

B
Bible Focus

> *The fruit of the Spirit is love, joy, peace, longsuffering,*
> *kindness, goodness, faithfulness, gentleness, self-control.*
> *Against such there is no law. And those who are Christ's have*
> *crucified the flesh with its passions and desires. If we live in*
> *the Spirit, let us also walk in the Spirit (Galatians 5:22–25).*

In giving the Galatians a character portrait of the godly life, the apostle
Paul was also giving the Galatians a portrait of the Holy Spirit! The character traits produced in the Christian are the traits *of the Spirit.* These are the
same character traits of Christ Jesus, and of God the Father. God's nature is
what is being replicated in the person who believes in Jesus and seeks to be
led by the Spirit. The fruit that is born in the believer's life is fruit that the
Spirit produces. It is not fruit that can be manufactured by the believer's
will, intellect, desire, or effort. It is fruit that is produced as a person "walks
in the Spirit" and seeks to be led by the Spirit.

Three things about this "fruit of the Spirit" are important for our consider-
ation:

First, this fruit is spiritual in nature. It truly is fruit *of the Spirit.* In other
words, circumstances do not affect the heart that is controlled by the Spirit.
As an example, the love produced by the Spirit is God's love, not brotherly
love or sexual love. The self-control is not man-mustered self-control, but
self-control enabled by the Spirit—God giving the *power* as man yields his
will, which produces genuine godly willpower. Very specifically:

LOVE— "agape" love, God's love that always seeks the highest good for a
person, no matter what that person may do to insult, injure, reject, or
humiliate.

JOY—an internal exuberance that rises from a relationship with God, and is
abiding—not dependent upon circumstances or external conditions
(which is happiness).

PEACE—serenity based upon belief that God is in control of all things at
all times

PATIENCE—slow to seek vengeance or become angry with other people,
trusting God to do His work in their lives and your own life

KINDNESS—a sweetness of spirit that allows relationships to develop and
flourish

GOODNESS—the application of God's love and care in practical ways for
the benefit of others

FAITHFULNESS—reliability and trustworthiness, knowing that God is always reliable and trustworthy

GENTLENESS—also translated in some versions as meekness, indicating that a person has sought to be tamed and brought under control by the Spirit, so that the person no longer reflects excessive or inappropriate anger or "wildness"

SELF-CONTROL—mastery, with God's help, over compulsive desires for pleasure and self-gratification

Second, the fruit of the Spirit is singular. Paul cites works of the flesh (plural)—indicating that these works can be done in isolation, and that they do not necessarily cluster together. However, he writes that the fruit of the Spirit is *not* plural. These character attributes do not function independently. They are a cluster of attributes that cannot be divided. One cannot have a little bit of love, a lot of joy, and no gentleness. To have the Spirit is to bear the fruit of the Spirit—all of the attributes to some degree.

Third, "fruit" benefits the believer and those that he or she encounters. All of these character attributes are for the good of the believer. They do not limit a believer or strain a believer's relationship with others—rather, they enhance and enlarge the believer's life and build up a believer's relationships. When expressed, they always build up the church.

It may be possible for a person, in his own human ability and strength, to reflect a loving or kind attitude from time to time, to engage in good works from time to time, or to bless others from time to time. It is impossible to sustain these character qualities, and to sustain *all* of them simultaneously, without the indwelling presence of the Spirit.

It may be possible for a person to feel that he "is an ounce short on patience" or a "quart low on joy," but God's Word tells us that any lack of character virtue is not a matter of an isolated deficiency of one godly attribute—rather, it reflects the truth that the person has not crucified his old nature (5:24). Our prayer must not become fractured—praying, for example, for "more peace" or "more faithfulness." Rather, our prayer must be, "Help me, God, to walk in the Spirit and to be led by the Spirit and to live in the Spirit!" You see, "if the Spirit is the source of our life, (we must) let the Spirit also direct our course" (5:25 NEB). If we want more fruit of the Spirit to be displayed *through* our lives, we must allow the Spirit freedom to work *in* our lives.

The key questions for every believer to ask are these:

Am I reflecting the fruit of the Spirit?

Am I "living" in the Spirit, "walking" in the Spirit, being "led" by the Spirit?

No person can live a godly life on his own strength.

But the Holy Spirit can enable every believer to live a godly life and reflect God's nature.

A
Application for Today

"It's too hard," the three-year-old girl said, and promptly sat down on the curb. She had been walking in her neighborhood with her older brother and father for about twenty minutes and had been struggling to keep pace, even though they were walking slowly. Finally, she had reached her limit.

Her father said, "Do you want me to carry you?"

The little girl put up both arms immediately, eager to have her father lift her high and put her on his shoulders.

From her perch on Dad's shoulders, she said, "It's a lot easier walking up here."

So it is with the Spirit.

In our own strength, we are limited, and we often tire easily in frustration at trying to live a godly life.

Is today the day when you need to cry out to the Lord, "I can't do this any longer. I'm not capable. Please help me!"

S
Supplementary Scriptures to Consider

Jesus said this about fruit:

> Either make the tree good and its fruit good, or else make the tree bad and its fruit bad; for a tree is known by its fruit. . . . For out of the abundance of the heart the mouth speaks. A good man out of the good treasure of his heart brings forth good things, and an evil man out of the evil treasure brings forth evil things (Matthew 12:33–35).

- Our character bears fruit in the form of words and deeds. Audit your own speech. Evaluate, while recalling specific events and relationships, whether your words or deeds in the last 48 hours have been:
LOVING —
JOYFUL —
PEACE-PRODUCING —
PATIENT —
KIND —
GOOD —
FAITHFUL —
GENTLE —
CONTROLLED —

- As you reflected on the past two days, how did your character measure up? Did you walk in the Spirit? How would a close friend evaluate your life based on this list? If you have children, what would they say?

The Bible tells us that the character we exhibit—through words and deeds—affects the quality of our own life, and the lives of others around us:

The fruit of the righteous is a tree of life (Proverbs 11:30).

- Recall a person whom you consider to be a righteous person. How does this person display his character traits and values? How do his words and actions produce life? How do his words and actions reflect the character traits of God (the fruit of the Spirit)?

- How does your reflecting the fruit of the Spirit influence the lives of others— specifically their attitude, speech, and behavior?

I

Introspection and Implications

1. How do you respond to this statement: "Those who are Christ's have crucified the flesh with its passions and desires"? How are fleshly passions and desires "crucified"?

2. What does it mean to you to "walk in the Spirit"?

3. As you read through Paul's list of "fruit of the Spirit," do you feel a conviction, "I need more of that"? Have you asked the Holy Spirit specifically to impart more of Himself to you? Have you asked Him to show you how best to manifest specific character traits?

C
Communicating the Good News

Too often we fail to ask in prayer for God to impart more of His nature to us. Very often we do not *have* more of God's character likeness because we have not asked—with active faith—for God to make us more like Christ Jesus. Why is it important in our efforts to win the lost that we ask the Spirit to lead us daily, and to reflect His life through us?

LESSON #6

BEARING BURDENS AND LOADS

Burden: something difficult to deal with or carry; nearly impossible for one person to handle
Loads: an amount that can be handled or carried by one person at any one time

B
Bible Focus

> *Bear one another's burdens, and so fulfill the law of*
> *Christ . . . But let each one examine his own work, and then*
> *he will have rejoicing in himself alone, and not in another. For*
> *each one shall bear his own load (Galatians 6:2,4).*

In just a few words, the apostle Paul brings resolution to an issue of
balance and concern that every person faces: to what extent is a person
responsible for others, and to what extent is each person responsible for
himself?

Two very different words are found in this brief passage: burden and load.

A burden is something that has oppressive, crushing power in a person's
life. It would be as if a boulder had fallen upon a person—with the potential
to kill or cause serious devastation. A burden is a trouble or difficulty too
large to be lifted, carried, or moved by one person. The burden may be an
external emergency—such as a flood that washes away a person's home. It
may be a serious illness or financial crisis that strikes an entire family. The
burden may also be a deep concern for the spiritual welfare of a loved one.

We need to *help* others when we see that they are crushed by burdens. We
need to cry out for help from others when we have burdens. There is no
shame in asking for help or receiving help in times of overwhelming crisis.
People need the loving arms, medical attention, practical provision, financial
assistance, and prayer support of others as they face times of intense personal need.

The vast majority of burdens are temporary. They have a "life span"—
perhaps days, perhaps weeks or months. Boulders are lifted and removed
from life's pathway, or from a person's shoulders or heart, through the
efforts of those who surround the person and form a loving team committed
to burden-lifting and boulder-busting. We are to help another person with his
burden until it is removed and ceases to be a burden.

In contrast, the word "load" in this passage refers to what might be
carried in a backpack or knapsack. Every person has a set of chores and
obligations that are a part of his daily routine and relationships. Every
person has responsibility for his own physical body, character traits, development of talents, thoughts and attitudes, speech and behavior, beliefs and
values, personal finances and purchases, and use of time.

Loads are daily and ongoing. They are to be carried individually.

We fulfill what God asks of us when we help others with the problems
that they cannot resolve on their own. In like manner, it is to our benefit to
ask for the help of other believers when we face problems that we cannot

resolve by ourselves. Our response in the face of a burden is: "Let us deal with this together, with God's help!"

We also fulfill what God asks of us when we take responsibility for dealing with life's daily problems that we *can* resolve or handle on our own. And we fulfill God's plan when we require others to take responsibility for those things that they can and should do for themselves. Our response in the face of a load is: "I shall handle this, with God's help; because without Him, I can do nothing of eternal value" (John 15:5).

We are to work together for the mutual benefit of the Body of Christ.

We are to develop our own lives so that we are able to contribute more to the kingdom of God.

Ask yourself today: In which areas of my life do I need to take more responsibility? In what ways do I need to allow others to take greater responsibility for their own lives?

Ask yourself today: Are there ways in which I can help another believer carry a burden in his life? Would I be wise to seek help from others in an area of my own life?

A
Application for Today

The man had been off work for four months after a serious automobile accident in which he had suffered several broken bones and internal injuries. After major surgery and a few days in intensive care, he had been hospitalized for more than two weeks. Once at home, he had faced long days of rest and several hours each day of painful but helpful rehabilitation therapy.

His wife, a loving and willing caregiver, had not only helped her husband physically, but had been a source of ongoing encouragement to him. She rallied members of their church to help pray for her husband's full recovery. The church members had also come to the aid of the family in providing meals, helping with yard care, and even providing some financial assistance with bills that the family's insurance policy hadn't covered. The man's physicians still anticipated that he would need two to three more months of rehab before he could return to work, but they were also pleased with the tremendous progress that he had made thus far.

One day the wife heard her husband call for her assistance from the living room of their home. She paused from the chore she was doing in the kitchen and prepared to go to his aid when she suddenly thought, *I don't think he really needs my help to do what he wants me to do right now. He is stronger than he thinks he is. He just doesn't know it. He has become so dependent on me to help him that he has stopped trying to help himself.* Rather than go to his aid, she quietly opened the kitchen door and went outside into their yard.

A few minutes later when she went back into the house, she found her husband standing at the kitchen sink. "You didn't come when I called you," he said with a tone of accusation.

"What did you need?" she asked innocently, pretending not to have heard his request.

"I wanted you to fill my water pitcher with ice and water," he said grumpily as he turned on the tap to add water to the pitcher that he had already filled with ice.

"Why did you want *me* to do it?" she asked sweetly.

He suddenly was aware of where he was standing and what he was doing! "Because you make such an excellent pitcher of ice water," he said with a grin.

"So do you," she said. "And that isn't all you are going to get to do for yourself."

Are you doing something for somebody today that the person *can* do for himself or herself? By "helping," are you actually hindering the person from full recovery or from personal growth? By "helping," are you keeping the other person from emotional maturity or spiritual responsibility? How can you encourage people to grow and mature in their walk with God?

S
Supplementary Scriptures to Consider

Paul reminded the Galatians of the teachings of Jesus:

> For the law is fulfilled in one word, even in this: "You shall
> love your neighbor as yourself" (Galatians 5:14).

- Do you love yourself? What are the words you would use to describe a healthy "self love"?

• Do you have difficulty loving others as yourself? In what ways?

• Sometimes we struggle in our attempts to determine the best way to "love" a neighbor. How do you decide when to express love to a neighbor? How do you decide the best way to express your love?

Paul warned about what can easily happen when we *fail* to love others as ourselves and fail to help them carry their burdens:

> But if you bite and devour one another, beware lest you be consumed by one another (Galatians 5:15)!

• What is the end result of competition in the church?

- What is the end result of ongoing, unyielding criticism in any relationship?

Paul concluded his discourse on walking in the Spirit with the statement below. To be conceited is to have an excessively high opinion of one's own qualities or abilities. To provoke is to exasperate others, make them irritable, or stir up their anger. At the root of envy is a competitive, striving attitude that seeks to control, manipulate, or possess another person or what they have.

> Let us not be conceited, provoking one another, envying one another (Galatians 5:26).

- How does conceit keep us from loving others and helping them with generosity?

- In what ways do we tend to "provoke" others in the church? Is there a difference between intentionally seeking to provoke others and unintentionally acting in a way that provokes? Is the net effect different?

• How does envy work against loving help?

Paul wrote specifically about ways that we are to help others who yield to temptation and sin:

> Brethren, if a man is overtaken in any trespass, you who are spiritual restore such a one in a spirit of gentleness, considering yourself lest you also be tempted (Galatians 6:1).

• We often say that one of the ways we help others is by "speaking the truth in love." What is required for a person to speak truth in love, or to admonish a person with a spirit of gentleness

• How are we to help a person bear the burden of a sinful or unhealthful addiction?

Paul gave this insight into how we personally are to carry our "backpack" loads:

> Let us lay aside every weight, and the sin which so easily ensnares us, and let us run with endurance the race that is set before us, looking unto Jesus, the author and finisher of our faith (Hebrews 12:1–2).

• What contributes to the "weight" of a load that we bear personally?

• As we carry our own loads, how can we make our "backpacks" lighter?

What must we lay aside permanently? What may be beneficial to lay aside temporarily?

• How important is it to seek God's forgiveness from sin and to ask for the Spirit's help in overcoming temptation?

• What does the phrase "author and finisher of our faith" mean to you? How does this give you courage as you deal with your daily obligations and responsibilities? How does this help you as you seek to grow spiritually, even in the face of loads and burdens?

I
Introspection and Implications

1. How do you discern the difference between a burden and a load?

2. How do you determine which burdens to help carry? Can you help a person bear a burden if the person does not want help, or does not perceive a problem to be a genuine burden?

3. When does helping turn into enabling?

4. In what ways might "doing for others" stunt their growth toward emotional and spiritual maturity?

C
Communicating the Good News

Every person has burdens from time to time. Every person has a "load" in life to carry. How are our evangelistic soul-winning efforts enhanced when we reach out to help others carry their burdens?

What is the role in evangelism of challenging a person to take personal responsibility for his own spiritual destiny, and for making his own personal decision about Jesus as his Savior?

LESSON #7

SOWING AND REAPING

Due season: the normal time for a seed, after being planted, to germinate, grow into a plant, and produce a harvest

B
Bible Focus

> *Do not be deceived, God is not mocked; for whatever a*
> *man sows, that he will also reap. For he who sows to his flesh*
> *will of the flesh reap corruption, but he who sows to the Spirit*
> *will of the Spirit reap everlasting life. And let us not grow*
> *weary while doing good, for in due season we shall reap if we*
> *do not lost heart. Therefore, as we have opportunity, let us do*
> *good to all, especially to those who are of the household of the*
> *faith (Galatians 6:7–10).*

Paul was not the first to teach about a universal "law of reciprocity." In today's terms, Paul may have said, "What goes around, comes around." The Galatians were familiar with this concept as it applied to moral law. The Greeks believed in Nemesis, the goddess of punishment and vengeance—and that a man who committed an evil deed immediately had Nemesis on his trail, and was eventually caught by Nemesis. Greek tragedies were grounded on the statement, "The doer shall suffer."

Jesus had taught in a parable about a man who sowed good seed, only to have his enemy sow bad seed in the same field. Both types of seed produced an expected harvest, and in the end, the harvest of tares was gathered up, bound in bundles, and burned. The harvest of wheat was gathered for future use (See Matthew 13:24–30).

Paul wove these two strains of teaching into one of the broader themes of his letter to the Galatians: The natural world and the spiritual world produce *different* harvests. What is sown in the fleshly realm is reaped in the fleshly realm as corruption. All evil deeds of the flesh result in a downward spiral that ends in death. Paul had also written this to the Romans: "The wages of sin is death" (Romans 6:23).

Conversely, those things that are sown in the spiritual realm produce an everlasting benefit—a blessing that begins now and spirals upward into an eternal life of pure blessing. Paul also wrote to the Romans, "The gift of God is eternal life" (Romans 6:23).

Therefore, Paul admonished, choose to sow the behaviors and words that reflect God's highest and best. Three additional lessons are embedded in this passage:

First, a person may receive forgiveness of past sins and the gift of eternal life upon accepting Jesus as Savior, but Christianity does not teach that all *consequences for past sins* are erased upon conversion. Earthly scars remain on earthly bodies. A life of debauchery cannot be erased. Decades of unhealthful habits, the infliction of ongoing pain, or neglect and abuse—physical, moral, or spiritual—cannot be negated.

Trends may be *reversed.*

Broken relationships may be *restored.*

Life may be *renewed.*

Eternal life may be *rewarded.*

But the consequences of earthly living are not always *erased* on this earth.

This is a sobering truth that needs to be shared fully and without a glossy coating to the next generation.

Second, not all consequences appear immediately. A person who sows to the Spirit may still suffer on this earth—a reward awaits, nonetheless, for both the good seeds sown *and* for faithfulness in suffering. The same is true for seeds of corruption. Negative consequences may not be experienced immediately or even in the near future for evil behavior and ongoing bad habits. Consequences *will* emerge over time.

Third, there is a "due season" appointed by God for all seeds planted to turn into a harvest. We are to plant practical seeds of service with generosity, and reflect the fruit of the Spirit consistently in thought, word, and deed, confident that eventually all seeds of godly behavior will produce a good harvest. God cannot be fooled. God's law cannot be made null or void.

What kinds of seeds are you sowing?

A
Application for Today

"My seeds aren't growing," an eight-year-old boy complained to his mother.

"You only planted that row of radish seeds a few days ago," Mom replied. "How do you know they aren't growing?"

"I dug up three of them. They looked just the same as when I planted them," the boy said.

"It takes a while for seeds to sprout and grow," Mom said. "Bury those seeds again and be patient."

It is difficult for most eight-year-old boys to be patient. A week later the boy went to his mother with a tiny sprout connected to a somewhat bulging but straight root. "My seeds are growing, but they aren't turning into radishes," the boy said.

Mom took one look at the radish sprout in her son's hand and said, "You haven't waited long enough."

More time passed. The boy dug up another radish sprout and came back to Mom with a new complaint, "My radishes are wimpy. Look how small this radish is. The seeds must have been bad."

"No," Mom said. "You just haven't waited long enough—give your row of radishes a little more time."

When harvest day finally came, the boy was thrilled on the one hand to have nice, round, red radishes, but disappointed that he had so few. Mom laughed lightly at his complaint. "You have so few radishes because you kept digging them up," she said. "Next year, let all the seeds grow until they are finished growing!"

Many times we think that the good seeds that we are sowing into the lives of others are having no effect. Or we regard the results as being vastly different than what was desired. At other times, we are disappointed that our harvest is meager, even though our seeds have been many.

God has a *due* season for all acts of loving kindness that we sow into the lives of others. He governs the growing season for each seed, and the amount of the harvest. Trust God truly to *be* the Lord of the Harvest! (See Luke 10:2.)

What harvest do you desire in your life?

What seeds are you planting that might produce such a harvest?

S
Supplementary Scriptures to Consider

God's promise of a harvest is sure:

> He who sows righteousness will have a sure reward
> (Proverbs 11:18).

• What does it mean to you to "sow righteousness"? Use your concordance to find other passages that describe "sowing righteousness."

• What does the phrase "sure reward" mean to you?

• Is there ever an instance when this is not true? How do you know?

The sowing of God's Word can be trusted to produce God's desired harvest:

> For as the rain comes down, and the snow from heaven,
> And do not return there,
> But water the earth,
> And make it bring forth and bud,
> That it may give seed to the sower
> And bread to the eater,
> So shall My word be that goes forth from My mouth;
> It shall not return to Me void,
> But it shall accomplish what I please,
> And it shall prosper in the thing for which I sent it
> (Isaiah 55:10–11).

- Man can sow seeds, but only God can make a seed grow. How is our faith tied to our sowing of God's Word? How is our faith tied to our doing practical good deeds?

- Are you ever frustrated that you cannot govern the laws related to sowing and reaping? Do you experience frustrations regarding God's law of reciprocity? How are you handling those frustrations?

- Can you recall an experience in your life in which you reaped a harvest long after you thought a harvest was impossible? Why do you think God sometimes delays a harvest, or prolongs a "growing season"?

- What harvests are you trusting God to produce in your life?

I
Introspection and Implications

1. Has God given you seeds to plant in someone's life? Are you "planting with generosity and expecting a harvest"?

2. Paul admonished the Galatians not to grow weary while doing good. How difficult is it to continue to do good if you don't see an immediate reward? If you don't see even the potential for a reward in your lifetime?

3. Paul wrote to the Galatians that they should remain assured that they would reap a harvest from sowing good if they didn't "lose heart." What does it mean to you to "lose heart"? How might "losing heart" keep a person from reaping a harvest?

C
Communicating the Good News

Even if you have only a limited time to share the Gospel message with another person, what can you trust God to do with the words that you speak?

Paul wrote to the Corinthians, "I planted, Apollos (a fellow minister of the Gospel) watered, but God gave the increase. So then neither he who plants is anything, nor he who waters, but God gives the increase. Now he who plants and he who waters are one, and each one will receive his own reward according to his own labor" (1 Corinthians 3:6–8). Do these verses encourage you or discourage you in your outreach to lost souls? Why?

NOTES TO LEADERS
OF SMALL GROUPS

A s the leader of a small discussion group, think of yourself as a facilitator with three main roles:

- Get the discussion started

- Involve every person in the group

- Encourage an open, candid discussion that remains Bible focused

Much of your role is to be a person who asks guided questions:

- What really impacted you most in this lesson?

- Was there a particular part of the lesson, or a question, that you found troubling?

- Was there a particular part of the lesson that you found encouraging or insightful?

- Was there a particular part of the lesson that you'd like to explore further?

Express to the group at the outset of your study that your goal as a group is to gain new insights into God's Word—this is not the forum for defending a point of doctrine or a theological opinion. Stay focused on what God's Word says and means. The purpose of the study is also to share insights on how to apply God's Word to everyday life. *Every* person in the group can and should contribute—the collective wisdom that flows from Bible-focused discussion is often very rich and deep.

Seek to create an environment in which every member of the group feels free to ask questions of other members in order to gain greater understanding. Encourage the group members to voice their appreciation to one another for new insights gained, and to be supportive of one another personally. Take the lead in doing this. Genuinely appreciate and value the contributions made by each person.

You may want to begin each study by having one or more members of the group read through the section provided under "Bible Focus." Ask the group specifically if it desires to discuss any of the questions under the "Application" section . . . the "Supplemental Scriptures" section . . . and the "Implications" and "Communicating the Gospel" section. If you do not come to a definitive conclusion or consensus—about any one question asked in this study,, encourage your group to dig deeper in order to have a satisfactory Bible-based answer. Challenge them to spend time before the next session in prayer regarding this issue. In addition, challenge each member to search the Scriptures to find the answer. Remember the words of Jesus: "Ask, and it will be given to you, seek, and you will find; knock, and it will be opened to you. For everyone who asks receives, and he who seeks finds, and to him who knocks it will be opened" (Matthew 7:7–8).

Finally, open and close your study with prayer. Ask the Holy Spirit, whom Jesus called the Spirit of Truth, to guide your discussion and to reveal what is of eternal benefit to you individually and as a group. As you close your study, ask the Holy Spirit to seal to your remembrance what you have read and studied, and to show you ways in the upcoming days, weeks, and months *how* to apply what you have studied to your daily life and relationships.

General Themes for the Lessons

Each lesson in this study has one or more core themes. Continually pull the group back to these themes. You can do this by asking simple questions, such as, "How does that related to _____ ?" "How does that help us better understand the concept of _____ ?" "In what ways does that help us apply the principle of _____ ?"

A summary of general themes or concepts in each lesson is provided below:

Lesson #1
ONLY ONE GOSPEL
Guarding against heresies and false teachings
Works of religion vs. grace of relationship
Doing things perfectly vs. being made whole by God

Lesson #2
JUSTIFIED BY FAITH
Peer pressure

Hypocrisy

Lesson #3
CHILDREN AND HEIRS
God's family—who is a part of it, God's design for its function

A godly inheritance

Privileges of the believer

Privilege within the Body of Christ

Earning and achieving vs. receiving from God

Lesson #4
THE WORKS OF THE FLESH
Man's fleshly/natural nature

The nature of evil deeds

"Practice" that produces habits

The negative impact of provocation

The negative impact of conceit

Lesson #5
THE FRUIT OF THE SPIRIT
Replication of God's own nature

Character

The impact of character upon what a person says and does

Walking in the Spirit

Being led by the Spirit

Living in the Spirit

Lesson #6
BEARING BURDENS AND LOADS
Burdens

Loads

Helping vs. enabling

Personal responsibility vs. corporate responsibility

Lesson #7
SOWING AND REAPING

Reciprocity

Consequences—for good or bad

Eternal rewards vs. earthly rewards

Due seasons

God's governance of all phases of seed-growing and harvest

Evangelism

NOTES

NOTES

NOTES

NOTES

NOTES

NOTES

NOTES

NOTES

CPSIA information can be obtained at www.ICGtesting.com
Printed in the USA
LVOW081916250812

295925LV00005B/11/P

A Note to Parents

DK READERS is a compelling prog
designed in conjunction with leadir
including Dr. Linda Gambrell, Profe
Clemson University. Dr. Gambrell h   as President of
the National Reading Conference and the College Reading
Association, and the International Reading Association.

Beautiful illustrations and superb full-color photographs
combine with engaging, easy-to-read stories to offer a fresh
approach to each subject in the series. Each DK READER is
guaranteed to capture a child's interest while developing his
or her reading skills, general knowledge, and love of reading.

The five levels of DK READERS are aimed at different
reading abilities, enabling you to choose the books that are
exactly right for your child:

Pre-level 1: Learning to read
Level 1: Beginning to read
Level 2: Beginning to read alone
Level 3: Reading alone
Level 4: Proficient readers

The "normal" age at which a child
begins to read can be anywhere
from three to eight years old.
Adult participation through
the lower levels is very helpful
for providing encouragement,
discussing storylines, and
sounding out unfamiliar words.

No matter which level you select,
you can be sure that you are helping
your child learn to read, then
read to learn!

LONDON, NEW YORK, MUNICH,
MELBOURNE, AND DELHI

Author Michele R. Wells
Senior Editor Ros Walford
Senior Art Editor Ann Cannings
Senior DTP Designer David McDonald
Production Controller Sophie Argyris
Proofreader Cecile Landau
Associate Publisher Nigel Duffield

Reading Consultant
Deborah Lock

First American Edition, 2012

Published in the United States by DK Publishing
375 Hudson Street, New York, New York 10014

10 9 8 7 6 5 4 3
003–184665–Jun/2012

Copyright © 2012 Dorling Kindersley Limited

Published in Great Britain by Dorling Kindersley Limited

DK books are available at special discounts when purchased in bulk
for sales promotions, premiums, fund-raising, or educational use.
For details, contact: DK Publishing Special Markets, 375 Hudson
Street, New York, New York 10014
SpecialSales@dk.com

A catalog record for this book is available
from the Library of Congress.

ISBN: 978-0-7566-9386-2

Color reproduction by Media Development & Printing Ltd., U.K.
Printed and bound in the U.S.A. by Lake Book Manufacturing, Inc.

The publisher would like to thank the following for their kind
permission to reproduce their photographs:
a=above, b=below/bottom, c=center, l=left, r=right, t=top

The publisher would like to thank the following for their kind
permission to reproduce their photographs:
(a-above; b-below/bottom; c-center; f-far; l-left; r-right; t-top)
Alamy: Jack Maguire (25); **Dorling Kindersley:** Alex Wilson, ©
Dorling Kindersley, courtesy of the Charlestown Shipwreck and
Heritage Centre, Cornwall (47tl); Peter Hayman © The British
Museum (23br). **Jacket: Alamy:** Jack Maguire (front cover).
All other images © Dorling Kindersley
For further information see: www.dkimages.com

For Nathan and Colby Bavaro

Discover more at
www.dk.com

Contents

READERS

READING
3
ALONE

Ghost
Stories

Written by Michele R. Wells

DK

DK Publishing

How to Tell a Good Ghost Story

It's getting late. The moon is out. It's time for a good scare with some ghost stories! Ghost stories are best when they make you shiver and shake. You can make them scarier if you tell them well.

Turn Out The Lights

There's nothing better for a ghost story than a dark night and a campfire. But there are other ways to create a spooky mood, too!

Get your friends to sit in a circle. Turn off all the lights. If grown-ups are around, ask them to light candles. Sit down and hold a flashlight so that just your face is lit.

Speak Softly

The best way to tell a ghost story is to speak softly. If you are quiet, your friends will have to listen hard to what you're saying. Speak slowly, too. This adds to the suspense and gives them time to wonder what will happen next.

Don't Explain Too Much

Have you ever watched a movie that was scary until the monster or ghost appeared on screen? Often, what's in your mind is much scarier than anything you see. Don't use too many details when telling your story. Use just enough for your friends to get the idea—but leave the rest to their imaginations.

Make It Sound Real

Most ghost stories are made up of all kinds of spooky sounding things that don't exist in real life. What makes them scary is thinking these things could have really happened. If a story begins "This happened to my cousin's friend last year," it will be much scarier to hear than one that starts out "Once upon a time."

So try to add to the story. Use places you know in your town. If you are camping, think about saying that the story happened in that very campsite. Use the woods or lake nearby. Put in people you know. Adding real people or places will make your story sound scarier.

Look Them In The Eye

Look at each of your friends as you tell your story. They'll feel like you are speaking to them. This is what a good storyteller does.

Make It Your Own

The stories in this book are just ideas. They are a place to start. You may have heard versions of them before, because ghost stories are often told and retold everywhere. These stories are not very detailed. As you read each one, you can think about how to change it to make it scarier for your friends. First, make each story your own. Then, make it as scary as you can.

The Half-Moon

William had spent the day at the carnival with his friends. It was getting dark, and some of the tents were starting to close. The friends finished their popcorn and cotton candy. They drank one last soda and started for the exit. William had promised his mother that he would come straight home that night.

Near the gate was a strange, silvery tent. It was still open. William looked at his watch. He knew that he had to leave, but there was something interesting about that tent. It had a black-and-red flag flying from the top and seemed to be lit by an eerie glow. William just had to check out this tent.

William said goodbye to his
friends and ducked inside. There,
at a low table draped with a purple
cloth, sat an old woman. She didn't
have a crystal ball or a set of cards.
She wasn't surrounded by candles
or strange carvings. She wasn't
wearing mystical rings or necklaces.
In fact, she looked a bit like
William's grandmother.

She said she was there to
tell his fortune. He sat down
on the chair in front of her.
"Tonight," she told him,
"the half-moon will last
for many days." He
waited for her to say more,
but that was all. William
stood up and thanked her.
He wasn't going to be late after
all, but that fortune sure was
a disappointment.

William decided to cut through
an open field to get home. When he
was halfway across it, the moon came
out from behind the clouds. It was
a half-moon, just as the woman had
said. What did she mean that it
would last for many days?

Just then, William tripped and
stumbled forward. He had come
across the top of an old well,
half-buried in the long grass.
He reached out to grab on to
something—anything—and
caught the edge of an old,
metal lid as he tumbled down.
He fell a long way.

William waited for his eyes to adjust to the darkness. He had landed on something hard. He reached into his pocket and pulled out his cell phone. It was smashed into pieces. Now he couldn't phone for help. There was nothing else down there with him—no ladder, no water or food. There was no way to get out, and he was all alone.

He looked up again. The rusty, metal lid was pulled halfway across the opening of the well. Moonlight was streaming through the other half. The far-away opening itself looked like a half-moon.

The old woman had said that it would last for many days.

William heard a low, growling sound. He turned to see the bright eyes and twitching snout of a huge, hungry creature. It was only a few feet away.

He wasn't alone after all.

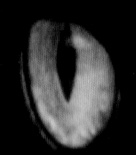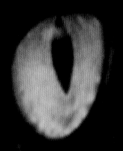

When the Clock Strikes Thirteen

Andrew was walking home after school one day, swinging his backpack. He had nothing special to do that afternoon, so he was not in much of a hurry. The sun was bright overhead, and there was a crisp fall breeze blowing.

He took a shortcut through an alley. The alley curved past the remains of a house that had recently burned down. There, he saw a boy about his age leaning up against the fence. The boy was tossing a baseball straight up in the air and catching it.

Andrew looked at the boy, and the boy looked back at Andrew. Andrew pulled his catcher's mitt from his backpack. Without a word, the boy picked up his bat and followed Andrew through the alley to the park on the other side.

They spent the day playing two-man baseball. Andrew had always been pretty good at batting and catching, but the boy, Jim, was just a little bit better. It was a great game. They played until the sun set, then played some more. One by one, the streetlights started turning on.

"I'd better get home," Andrew finally said to Jim. "Thanks for a great game." Jim shook his hand and told him he'd see Andrew around.

"Want to play again tomorrow?" Andrew asked. Jim shook his head and said, "I'll see you next when the clock strikes thirteen." With that he grabbed his stuff and ran back through the alley.

Andrew's mother was reading the newspaper when he walked in. She said that there had been a terrible fire the week before. The house that had burned down was only a few blocks away. "Was the boy who died in your class?" she asked Andrew. "He was exactly your age."

Andrew thought for a minute. "I haven't heard anything about it at school," he said. "What was the boy's name?"

His mother looked back through the newspaper article. "His name was Jim," she said. "He was on the baseball team."

Andrew never saw the boy again, but he also never forgot Jim's final words. He always made sure that he was fast asleep well before midnight. He didn't want to take the chance that Jim would keep his promise.

People say that on a dark night— just like this one—you can hear Jim running the bases and laughing. Listen closely. What was that?

The Hand

Mark and Emma were two seniors from the high school down the road. One Friday evening, they went to see a horror film. When the movie ended, Mark asked if Emma wanted to take a drive. They went out to the woods on the edge of town.

They parked in a darkened spot. It was so heavily wooded that even the moonlight didn't come through the

branches. Mark turned off the engine, but left the radio on. He was looking for a good station. A breaking news report came on. The newscaster said that a patient with a hook for a hand had escaped from the local asylum. The police advised everyone to stay home and lock their doors and windows. The patient was extremely dangerous.

Emma wanted to go home, but Mark laughed at her. "You're just scared because we saw that horror movie tonight," he said. "There's nothing to worry about."

Suddenly, they heard a loud bang. It came from somewhere near the back of the car. Mark turned the lights back on and looked through the rearview mirror. He couldn't see anything. "It's probably just a branch that fell," he told Emma.

Another bang, louder than before, came from the back of the car. This bang shook the car so hard that it bounced up and down. Mark took off his seatbelt to go investigate. "It's too dark out there," cried Emma. "You won't see anything. Let's get out of here."

They sat quietly for a moment, listening. Just then, a rough, metallic scraping sounded overhead, as if someone—or something—was on top of the car. The sound moved slowly from the back of the car toward the front. It stopped when it was directly above them.

Mark turned the key and threw the car into reverse. He backed out of the spot so quickly that the tires spun wildly on the leafy ground. He raced back to Emma's house, then jumped out of the car. He wanted to make sure there was no damage.

He was staring at a strange set of dents in his rear bumper when he heard a loud scream.

Mark ran around the car to find Emma crying. She pointed in horror at her door handle.

Hanging from it was a bloody hook.

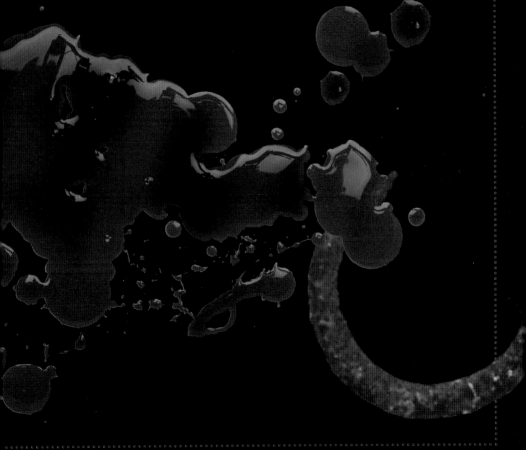

The Girl on the Road

Last winter, my cousin, Alex, was driving on a winding highway road near his home. It had just started to snow. The road was getting icy, so he slowed down. He didn't want to miss his exit.

As he neared his turn, he slowed down even more. He thought he saw a girl on the side of the road. It was very cold out, and the girl was wearing just a long, white dress. She didn't have a coat or scarf. She was shivering. It was late and there were no other cars on the road. Alex pulled over near the girl. He opened the door and asked if she needed some help.

The girl walked slowly over to the open door. Her hair was very blonde, and her eyes were so light they were almost colorless. Her skin was pale. There were snowflakes on her eyelashes. When she spoke, he had to listen hard to hear her voice over the howling of the wind.

She said her name was Ellen. She had been on her way home from a dance. She had gotten into an argument with her date, and had jumped out of the car. She had been walking home when it started to snow. She had left her coat in the car and was freezing.

Alex offered to take her home. Ellen smiled gratefully and got into the car. She said very little—only giving directions, such as "Turn here" and "Go through the next light." He turned the car's heater on high, but she kept shivering.

Finally, they turned down a dark road. Ellen pointed to a house on the opposite side of the street. She said it was her parents' home. The lights were out and no one seemed to be waiting up.

He unlocked the door and turned to open it for Ellen, but she was gone. There was nothing in the passenger's seat but a few melted streaks of snow.

Alex peered out in the snow but saw no sign of Ellen. Worried, he got out of the car to look for her. He ran up to her parents' house. Even though it was late, he rang the doorbell.

An elderly woman answered the door. She was dressed in a robe, and looked sleepy. The doorbell had woken her. Alex apologized for disturbing her. He said he had brought her daughter home. He asked if she had come inside.

"Did you pick her up on the highway?" the old woman asked.

Alex nodded. "She told me that she was on her way home from a dance."

The old woman sighed and pulled her robe tighter. "That was Ellen. She was on her way home from a dance five years ago. She got into a fight with her date and tried to walk home. A car slid on the icy road and hit her. She was killed."

Alex turned to look again at his car. The door was open, and light was streaming out.

The old woman continued, "And every year since, on this night, she tries again to get home. Thank you for picking her up."

The Third Door on the Left

Jake and Jennifer were upset. They didn't get to go to camp this summer with the rest of their friends. Instead, they had to stay with their great-aunt, Rose, in her rickety, old house by the lake.

The house was huge—way too big for just their aunt—and she was too old to be much fun. She didn't even own a television, never mind a computer or any video games! The lake was too cold for swimming, Aunt Rose didn't have a boat, and there was no one else their age who lived nearby. It was going to be a long summer.

After dinner the first night, Aunt Rose showed them around. Most of the rooms were plain. She made a big show of opening the door of the library on the second floor. "You may read anything you like in here," she said, "and go into any of the other rooms on this floor. However, you are not allowed to go near the third door on the left." Jennifer rolled her eyes. The books were old and dusty. They wouldn't be interesting.

For a week, Jake and Jennifer explored every room in the old house, looking for games or puzzles, or anything else that might be fun. One night, they had nothing to do. Aunt Rose was fast asleep by the fireplace. "Let's try the library," suggested Jake. They walked around the room. Jennifer read the titles of the books. They were collections of ghost stories! Maybe they wouldn't be so bad after all.

Jake and Jennifer each grabbed a book. They sat down on the cobwebby, old chairs and tried reading aloud to each other. Some of the books had missing pages, so they couldn't find out how the stories ended.

Others were so ancient that they just fell apart in their hands.

"This is dumb," Jake said after a while. "There's nothing to do in this place. Let's just go to sleep."

"I'm not tired," Jennifer replied. "And there's still one room we haven't checked out…"

They jumped up and ran to the door. They looked carefully up and down the hall. Aunt Rose was nowhere to be seen.

Slowly, Jake and Jennifer crept down the hallway. They stood in front of the third door on the left. It looked no different from any of the other doors in the house.

Jake put his hand out and slowly turned the knob. It wasn't even locked! He smiled at Jennifer and pushed open the door…

Aunt Rose finished her eggs alone the next morning. She made a cup of tea and washed the dishes. Then, she shuffled up the stairs to the second floor.

There, in front of the open door, stood Jake and Jennifer. Jake still had his outstretched hand on the doorknob. They were both standing completely still. Their hair had turned stark white, and they had looks of terror on their faces.

Aunt Rose shook her head and slowly returned downstairs.

The Shadow in the Mirror (or, Bloody Mary)

Long ago, there were deep, dark woods in this town. And in the woods lived a woman. No one had seen her for many years, but they heard her terrible singing late at night when the moon was full. People called her "Bloody Mary." They said that she liked to drink blood.

Parents warned their children not to stay out late during the full moon. Boys and girls who missed curfew on those nights would go missing. One by one, they would disappear. Their families searched everywhere. The police would bring dogs to sniff out their trails. The clues always ended where the woods began.

One night a boy named John stayed at school to play basketball. He lost track of the time, and didn't leave until well after dark. He had to pass by the woods on the way home. Suddenly, he began to scream.

A man was passing by in a car. He heard the screams, but could not find John. He saw an eerie green light in the trees. The light was all around Bloody Mary. She was singing. As he watched, she seemed to grow younger. Then she disappeared. John was never heard from again.

That night, people in the town had enough. They set the woods on fire. People said they heard Mary singing at first, then screaming. They said she died in the fire. The trees all burned down, but her house was still there. Behind it was a pile of bones. The bones were from all the missing children.

Mary had chopped them up. She had been drinking their blood to stay young.

There was nothing left inside the house except a cracked mirror and a piece of paper. On the paper was a warning. It said that Mary would come back someday. And this is how to bring her back:

Wait until midnight. Shut off all the lights. Look in a mirror, and repeat her name three times. Say "Bloody Mary, Bloody Mary, Bloody Mary." If you see a shadow behind you in the mirror, it's Mary. And you'd better run. She will be after your blood!

Man's Best Friend

Ever since Tommy was a little boy, his dog, Spike, had been there for him. Spike was Tommy's best friend. Whenever Tommy got scared or felt alone, Spike would curl up under his bed. Tommy would stretch his hand down and Spike would lick his fingers. Tommy was comforted, knowing that Spike was there. He would fall asleep smiling, glad that his dog was nearby.

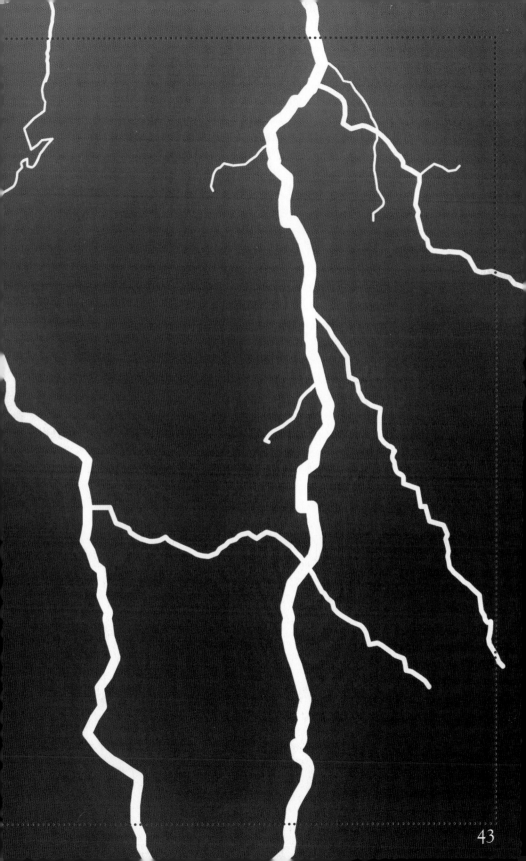

Now Tommy is
13 years old. He is too
old to get frightened by noises
during the night, and he doesn't feel
alone much anymore. However, on
this night a terrible thunderstorm was
raging outside. His parents were at
a wedding and wouldn't be home
until early morning. Tommy crawled
into bed but could not sleep. He

heard a soft whimper from under the bed. Tommy stretched his hand down. His dog began to lick his hand softly.

Tommy tossed and turned.
He put the pillow over his head.
He tried to fall asleep, despite the crashing thunder and crackling lightning. Finally, Tommy stretched his hand down beside the bed again. The dog's continued, soft licking and whimpering made him feel better. At last, he fell fast asleep.

His parents finally came home around three in the morning. They opened his bedroom door. Light streamed into his room. Groggily, Tommy sat up, wondering what was wrong. His parents never woke him up in the middle of the night.

"What do you mean by leaving the dog outside in the rain all night?" his father demanded.

Tommy started to protest, "Spike isn't outside. He's under my—"

Just then, the dog bounded into Tommy's room, soaked to the bone. He shook his body and the cold rain sprayed off his fur. He settled under Tommy's bed and began licking his hand.

Find Out More
Books

Creepy Campfire Tales
By James D. Adams
A collection of original, scary stories to
tell around the campfire. For ages 9 and up.

Scary Stories to Tell in the Dark
By Alvin Schwartz
Spine-tingling, classic tales of horror.
For ages 9 and up.

Ask the Bones
By Arielle North Olson and Howard Schwartz
This collection of scary folktales features stories
from many different cultures. For ages 8 and up.

Ghost Hunt: Chilling Tales of the Unknown
By Jason Hawes, Grant Wilson, and Cameron Dokey
This collection of scary stories is based on case files
from the Atlanta Paranormal Society, TAPS.
For ages 9 and up.

*Beware!: R. L. Stine Picks His Favorite
Scary Stories*
By R. L. Stine
Bestselling horror author R. L. Stine compiles stories
from Ray Bradbury, Bram Stoker, Edward Gorey, and
more in this read-aloud collection. For ages 8 and up.

Glossary

Ancient
Very old

Appear
To be or come
into sight

Asylum
A hospital or other
place where the sick
or mentally ill are
cared for

Cobwebby
Covered with cobwebs
or spider webs

Colorless
Without color; pale

Crept
Walked slowly
and quietly

Eerie
Strange and
frightening; creepy

Exist
To be found in
real life

Fortune
Chance or luck;
sometimes used to
mean future events

Groggily
Tiredly

Investigate
To look closely; to
discover the facts
of an event

Midnight
Twelve o'clock in
the morning; the time
when night officially
becomes day

Mood
An overall feeling

Mystical
Strange and
mysterious

Rickety
Old and unsteady;
likely to fall apart

Shuffled
Slowly sliding one's
feet along the ground
while walking

Suspense
A feeling of worry
or nervousness
about what will
happen next

Whimper
A low, whining sound